UNDERSTANDING
The Bible

The Story Of The New Testament

By the same author

BASIC CHRISTIANITY

YOUR CONFIRMATION

CONFESS YOUR SINS

THE EPISTLES OF JOHN: A COMMENTARY

THE CANTICLES AND SELECTED PSALMS

MEN MADE NEW

OUR GUILTY SILENCE

ONLY ONE WAY

ONE PEOPLE

CHRIST THE CONTROVERSIALIST

GUARD THE GOSPEL

BALANCED CHRISTIANITY

CHRISTIAN MISSION IN THE MODERN WORLD

BAPTISM AND FULLNESS

THE LAUSANNE COVENANT

CHRISTIAN COUNTER-CULTURE

UNDERSTANDING THE BIBLE   *Available in library
or paperback editions*

OTHER BOOKS IN THIS SERIES

THE PURPOSE AND THE PLACE

THE STORY OF THE OLD TESTAMENT

THE MESSAGE TO TRUST

THE BIBLE FOR TODAY

UNDERSTANDING
The Bible

The Story Of The New Testament

by   John R.W. Stott

Understanding the Bible

SCRIPTURE UNION

47 Marylebone Lane
London W1M 6AX

Published in the United States by
Regal Books Division, G/L Publications
Glendale, California 91209   U.S.A.

© Copyright John Stott 1978
First published in *Understanding The Bible* 1972
Reprinted 1972, 1973,
Revised 1976
First published in this form 1978

ISBN 0 85421 618 9

U.S. Library of Congress Catalog Card No. 501 7505
ISBN 0 8307 0659 3

Illustrations by Annie Valloton
Maps by Liz Leyland and Jenny Grayston

Printed in Great Britain by
McCorquodale (Newton) Ltd., Newton-le-Willows

PUBLISHER'S PREFACE

UNDERSTANDING THE BIBLE has appeared in several editions, not only in the United Kingdom, North America, Australia and India, but in such languages as German, Swedish, Dutch, Spanish, Faroese, Japanese, Chinese and Thai. The author's objectives set out in his preface are being steadily fulfilled.

Now we are issuing the original publication in five separate volumes in a further attempt to achieve those aims. We anticipate meeting an even wider need; making readily available to new readers the individual subjects on which the Rev. John R. W. Stott has written so clearly.

Their use will not be confined to the individual reader; it will be practicable to use them in study and house groups, etc.

Each book contains recommendations for further reading and an index of scripture references referred to in the text.

PREFACE

Every author owes it to the reading public to explain himself. Why has he thought fit to swell the torrent of books—especially religious books—which pours from the world's printing presses every day? Can he justify his rash enterprise? Let me at least tell you frankly the kind of people I have had in mind while writing. They fall into two categories.

First, the new Christian. With the spread of secularism in our day, an increasing number of people are being added to Christ and His Church who have no religious background whatever. Here, for example, is a young man from a non-Christian family. The Christian instruction he received at school was minimal, and possibly misleading. In any case the fashion was to pay no attention to it. He did not go to Sunday School as a kid, and he has seldom if ever been to church. But now he has found Christ, or rather been found by Him. He is told he must read the Bible daily if he is to grow into spiritual maturity. The Bible is a closed book to him, however—an unexplored, uncharted territory. Who wrote it, he asks, and when, where and why? What is its message? What is the foundation for its claim to be a 'holy' or special book, the book of God? And how is it to be read and interpreted? These are proper questions to ask, and some answer must be given to them before the new Christian can derive maximum benefit from his Bible reading.

Then, secondly, there is the Christian of several years' standing. In the main, he has been a conscientious Bible reader. He has read his portion faithfully every day. But somehow it has become a stale habit. The years have passed, and he himself has changed and matured as a person. Yet he has not developed as a Christian in any comparable way. A sign (and cause) of this is that he still reads the Bible as he did when he was a child, or a new convert. Now he is tired of his superficiality, his immaturity, and not a little ashamed. He longs to become an adult, integrated Christian, who knows and pleases God, fulfils himself in serving others and can commend the gospel in meaningful terms to a lost, bewildered generation.

My desire is to assure such a Christian that the secrets of Christian maturity are ready to be found in Scripture by all who seek them. There is a breadth to God's Word which few of us ever encompass, a depth which we seldom plumb.

In particular, our Christianity is mean because our Christ is mean. We impoverish ourselves by our low and paltry views of Him. Some speak of Him today as if He were a kind of syringe to be carried about in our pocket, so that when we are feeling depressed we can give ourselves a fix and take a trip into fantasy. But Christ cannot be used or manipulated like that. The contemporary Church seems to have little understanding of the greatness of Jesus Christ as lord of creation and lord of the Church, before whom our place is on our faces in the dust. Nor do we seem to see His victory as the New Testament portrays it, with all things under His feet, so that if we are joined to Christ, all things are under our feet as well.

It seems to me that our greatest need today is an enlarged vision of Jesus Christ. We need to see Him as the One in whom alone the fulness of God dwells and in whom alone we can come to fulness of life.[1]

There is only one way to gain clear, true, fresh, lofty views of Christ, and that is through the Bible. The Bible is the prism by which the light of Jesus Christ is broken into its many and beautiful colours. The Bible is the portrait of Jesus Christ. We need to gaze upon Him with such intensity of desire that (by the gracious work of the Holy Spirit) He comes alive to us, meets with us, and fills us with Himself.

In order to apprehend Jesus Christ in His fulness, it is essential to understand the setting within which God offers Him to us. God gave Christ to the world in a specific geographical, historical and theological context. More simply, He sent Him to a particular place (Palestine), at a particular time (the climax of centuries of Jewish history) and within a particular framework of truth (progressively revealed and permanently recorded in the Bible). So the following chapters are concerned with the geography, history, theology, authority and interpretation of the Bible. Their object is to present the setting within which God once revealed and now offers Christ, so that we may the better grasp for ourselves and share with others the glorious fulness of Jesus Christ Himself.

NOTE

1 See Col. 1.19; 2.9, 10

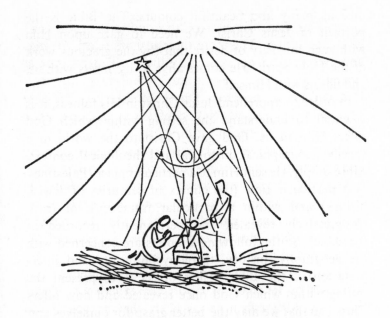

THE STORY OF THE NEW TESTAMENT

In Book 2 of this series the story of the Old Testament was sketched, covering several thousands of years. In this chapter an outline of the New Testament story will be given, covering less than a century. It is a fascinating tale of the words and deeds of Jesus of Nazareth, first of what He 'began to do and teach'[1] during His life on earth and then of what He continued to do and teach through His chosen apostles after He had returned to His Father and constituted His church.

The Four Gospels

Although there are a few scattered references to Jesus in contemporary secular writings, especially in Tacitus and Suetonius, the main source of our information about Him remains the four 'gospels'. They are rightly so called. For strictly speaking they are not biography, but testi-

1

mony. They bear witness to Christ and to the good news of His salvation. Therefore their authors select, arrange and present their material according to their purpose as 'evangelists'. This gives us no ground to doubt their trustworthiness, however. On the contrary, we should approach the gospels with confidence, not suspicion. There are many reasons for doing so.

First, the four evangelists were certainly Christian men, and Christian men are honest men to whom truth matters.

Secondly, they give evidence of their impartiality by including incidents they would clearly have preferred to omit. For example, although by that time Peter was a highly respected church leader, neither his boastfulness nor his denial of Jesus is suppressed.

Thirdly, they claim either to be themselves eye-witnesses of Jesus or to report the experience of eye-witnesses. Although it seems likely that no gospel was actually published earlier than A.D. 60, we must not imagine that there was an empty gap between the ascension of Jesus and that date. This was the period of 'oral tradition', in which the words and deeds of Jesus were used in Christian worship, evangelism and the teaching of converts, and so began to be collected in writing. Luke says he drew on 'many' such compilations.[2]

Fourthly, Jesus seems to have taught like a Jewish Rabbi. He gave His instruction in forms (e.g. parables and epigrams) which a tenacious oriental memory would have had no difficulty in learning by heart, and in addition He promised that the Holy Spirit would stimulate the apostles' memory.[3]

Fifthly, if God said and did something absolutely unique and decisive through Jesus, as Christians believe, it is inconceivable that He would have allowed it to be lost in the mists of antiquity. If He intended future generations to benefit from it, He must have made provision for it to be reliably reported, in order to make the good news available to all men in all times and places. What He decided to do was to present the one gospel in four gospels.

As we read the gospels it becomes clear that they tell the same story, yet differently. The first three (Matthew, Mark and Luke) are usually known as the 'synoptic' gospels because their stories run parallel and present a 'synoptic' (i.e. similar) account of Jesus' life. Matthew and Luke appear to have known Mark's gospel and to have incorporated most of it in theirs. They also have some additional common material, generally known as 'Q' (the first letter of the German word *Quelle*, a source), though each has independent information as well. Scholars are not agreed how far the Synoptic Gospels were known or used by John, but most believe that his gospel was the last to be published.

The gospel of Mark is the shortest and probably the earliest of the four. The style is terse, the stories are vivid and the tone is exciting, with everything happening 'immediately' after something else. The apostle Peter referred to Mark as his 'son',[4] and the second-century fathers Papias and Irenaeus described him as Peter's interpreter. It may well be, therefore, that Peter's memoirs or preaching or both have been preserved in Mark's gospel, which has obvious similarities to Peter's *First Letter*.

It is possible that Matthew's name became attached to the first gospel because 'Q', consisting largely of the sayings of Jesus, was his collection. We know he was a tax-collector,[5] so that he will have been used to making notes and keeping records. Certainly, according to Papias, 'Matthew compiled the *logia*—sayings—in Hebrew (i.e. Aramaic, the language spoken by Jesus), and everybody translated them as he was able'.[6] His gospel is very Jewish and betrays his special interest in the fulfilment of prophecy.

3

Luke is the only Gentile among the New Testament authors. He had himself travelled widely and as one of Paul's companions will have absorbed the apostle's teaching about God's grace to the Gentiles. Consequently, he emphasizes the universal scope of Christ's love, as illustrated in his care for the despised 'outsiders' of contemporary Judaism—women and children, publicans and sinners, lepers, Samaritans and Gentiles.

John had evidently meditated long and deeply on the teaching of Jesus. His own thought and language became so completely assimilated to his Lord's that it is not always easy to tell when the one's words end and the other's begin. He leaves us in no doubt about the purpose of his gospel, for he himself defines it for us. He has, he says, recorded a number of the 'signs' which Jesus did, so that readers will believe in Him as the Christ, God's Son, and so receive eternal life.[7] True to his avowed purpose he assembles a variety both of signs and of witnesses, in order to demonstrate the unique 'glory' of Jesus.

The Birth and Youth of Jesus

Each evangelist begins his story at a different place. Mark plunges almost immediately into Jesus' public ministry, heralded as it was by John the Baptist. John goes to the other extreme and reaches back into a past eternity to the pre-incarnate existence of Jesus Christ. As 'the Word' He was with God in the very beginning. Indeed, He was Himself God, and was active in the creation of the universe. Long before He actually 'came' into the world by becoming flesh, He was continually 'coming into the world' as the true light (though unrecognized) to enlighten every man with the light of reason and of conscience.[8]

It is Matthew and Luke who tell us the actual story of

Jesus' birth. Luke tells it through the eyes of the Virgin Mary (perhaps even from her own lips), while Matthew tells it from Joseph's point of view.

Luke records the angel's announcement to Mary that both her conception and the boy to be born will be supernatural:

'And the angel said to her, "the Holy Spirit will come upon you, and the power of the Most High will overshadow you; therefore the child to be born will be called holy, the Son of God." '9

Luke goes on to describe how Mary shared her secret with her cousin Elizabeth who was shortly to give birth to John the Baptist; how Joseph (whose painful dilemma over Mary's pregnancy Matthew describes) travelled south with her from Nazareth to Bethlehem their ancestral home, in order to comply with the requirements of the imperial census; and how it was in the stable of a Bethlehem inn that Jesus was born and laid by His mother in a manger.

Although the world's Saviour was born in such lowliness, and received no public acclaim, there were those who came to pay homage to Him. Luke tells of certain shepherds who learned the good news from angels, and Matthew of mysterious Magi—astrologer-priests from Persia—who were guided to Him by a star. There seems to have been a deliberate providence in bringing these two contrasting groups. For the shepherds were Jewish, untutored and poor, while the Magi were Gentile, cultured and rich. Yet the barriers of race, education and social rank were transcended by their common worship of the infant Christ. They foreshadow the colourful diversity of Christ's followers.

Not everybody worshipped Him, however. Herod the Great, who in the course of his reign murdered every possible rival, was alarmed to hear the Magi say they had come to honour the King of the Jews. For he was the king of the Jews. So who was this? Warned by God of Herod's resolve to destroy the child, Joseph and Mary fled with Him to the safety of Egypt, and the one who was born to rule became a refugee.

Jesus was brought up in Nazareth in Galilee. His home must have been far from affluent, for when presenting their firstborn son to the Lord, Joseph and Mary brought a pair of pigeons as their offering, prescribed in the law for those who could not afford a lamb. But it will have been a happy home, shared (as the years passed) by the other children of the family. Joseph worked as a carpenter and taught his trade to Jesus, while Mary will have nurtured Him in godliness and righteousness by teaching Him to read the Scriptures and to pray. In the beautiful countryside around He will have become familiar with the lilies of the field and the birds of the air, to which He later referred, and with the living God who clothes and feeds them.

The only incident from Jesus' boyhood which is recorded in the gospels took place when He reached the age of twelve and was taken up to Jerusalem for the Passover, to prepare at thirteen to become a 'son of the commandment'. After the festival He was accidentally left behind. His parents found Him 'sitting among the teachers, listening to them and asking them questions'. These Jewish leaders were 'amazed at His understanding and His answers', and His parents were perplexed when He asked them: 'Did you not know that I must be in My Father's house?' His sense of communion with God as Father and of compulsion to do His will were to remain with Him throughout His later ministry.

Apart from this story, recorded in Luke 2:41–51, the verses which immediately precede and follow it tell us all we need to know about Jesus' youth. Both are bridge verses, verse 40 spanning the twelve years from His birth and verse 52 the remaining 18 or so years before His public ministry began. Both tell us that during these years Jesus was developing naturally yet perfectly, in body, mind and spirit. Here is verse 52:

> 'And Jesus increased in wisdom and in stature, and in favour with God and man.'

Although the evangelists are not concerned to give us a strictly chronological account of the Lord's public ministry, it appears from John's gospel to have lasted approximately three years.[10] We may call the first the year of obscurity, the second the year of popularity and the third the year of adversity.

The Year of Obscurity

All four gospels recount something of the ministry of John the Baptist. He was an ascetic, wearing nothing but a camel's hair cloak with a leather girdle, and eating an austerity diet of locusts and wild honey. Through his lips, after a silence of several centuries, the authentic voice of prophecy was again heard, as he summoned the people to repentance and to his baptism of repentance in preparation for the coming of the Messiah. Large crowds flocked to the River Jordan to listen to his preaching and to be baptized.

When Jesus presented Himself for baptism John demurred, for he had pronounced himself unworthy even to stoop down and undo the sandal strap of the one coming after him. But Jesus was resolved to fulfil all righteousness and, though He had no sins of His own to confess, to identify Himself with the sins of others. So He persuaded John to baptize Him. At that moment the Holy Spirit came upon Him like a dove, and the Father's voice was heard proclaiming Him in words of Old

Testament Scripture both His beloved son and His suffering servant.[11]

Immediately after His baptism, the same Spirit who had descended upon Him 'drove' Him into the Judean desert. Here He fasted for forty days in order no doubt to seek strength through prayer for the ministry to which He had just been commissioned. During this period He was also savagely tempted to compromise with the devil by trying to attain right ends by wrong means. But the Lord's hidden years of Scripture meditation stood Him in good stead. He was able to counter every diabolical suggestion with an apt Biblical rejoinder. For He was determined to live according to Scripture and so obey His Father's will.

It appears that after the temptation Jesus returned to the River Jordan and gave the two brothers Andrew and Simon Peter a kind of preliminary call to His service. They left John the Baptist and began to follow Jesus.

Returning north to Galilee, Jesus performed His first miracle, changing water into wine at a wedding in Cana. It symbolized His claim to introduce a new order, and by it He 'manifested His glory, and His disciples believed in Him'.[12]

Next He went up to Jerusalem for the Passover and boldly ejected from the temple courts the merchants and money-changers who had profaned it. When challenged about His action, He replied enigmatically:

'Destroy this temple, and in three days I will raise it up'[13]

It was another dramatic claim about the new order. For He was alluding not only to His physical body which would be raised from death in three days, but to His spiritual body, the church, which would live in the power of the resurrection. His church would also be a new and spiritual temple, God's dwelling place, to replace Herod's material temple which would be destroyed.

One man who was deeply impressed by the early teaching and miracles of Jesus was a leading Jewish rabbi called Nicodemus. He came under cover of dark for a private interview, to be told by Jesus that the indispensable condition for seeing and entering God's kingdom was a new birth from above by the power of the Holy Spirit. Some time later on His way north again into Galilee, Jesus repeated this message or something very similar, though not now to a Jewish man, but to a Samaritan woman. She needed 'living water', He said, an inner 'spring of water welling up to eternal life', which would quench her thirst and which only He could supply.[14]

Other details of the first year of Jesus' ministry are not recorded. Most of it seems to have been spent in Judea. It was a transition period, during which His ministry overlapped with the ministry of His forerunner, John the Baptist. The disciples of Jesus were also baptizing. And gradually those following Jesus came to outnumber those following John, which John accepted with beautiful humility, saying:

'He must increase, but I must decrease.'[15]

But this situation was the signal for Jesus to leave Judea for Galilee. Soon afterwards John was arrested and imprisoned, and the Galilean ministry, the year of popularity, began.[16]

The Year of Popularity

Attending the synagogue service one sabbath day in His home town Nazareth, Jesus was given the scroll of Isaiah from which to read:

'The Spirit of the Lord is upon Me, because He has

anointed Me to preach good news to the poor. He has sent Me to proclaim release to the captives and recovering of sight to the blind, to set at liberty those who are oppressed, to proclaim the acceptable year of the Lord'.[17]

During the sermon which followed, Jesus dared to claim that He was Himself the fulfilment of this Scripture. At first the congregation were amazed at His gracious words. But when He went on to suggest that His ministry, like that of the prophets Elijah and Elisha, would be more acceptable to the Gentiles than to Israel, they were so infuriated that they drove Him out of the city and tried even to push Him over the nearby hill. It was a foretaste of His coming rejection, and forced Him to move His home and headquarters from Nazareth to Capernaum on the north-west shore of the lake.

From Capernaum during the rest of this second year Jesus made innumerable journeys throughout Galilee. Matthew sums up what form His ministry took:

'And He went about all Galilee, teaching in their synagogues and preaching the gospel of the kingdom and healing every disease and every infirmity among the people.'[18]

First, He preached. Mark says that the topic of His preaching was 'the gospel of God', summarized in these words:

'The time is fulfilled, and the kingdom of God is at hand; repent, and believe in the gospel.'[19]

This divine kingdom was the personal reign of God in the lives of men, and He (Jesus) had come to inaugurate it. Its arrival was in fulfilment of Old Testament expectation, and in order to 'receive', 'enter' or 'inherit' the kingdom men must repent and believe, humbly accepting

10

its privileges and submitting to its demands like little children.

Next, He taught. That is, He did more than announce the gospel of the kingdom and call men to enter it; He went on to teach His disciples the law of the kingdom. Of this we have no better summary than the 'Sermon on the Mount', consisting no doubt of instruction given over a protracted period. Its integrating theme is the call to His disciples to be different from both pagans and Pharisees. 'Do not be like them', He said. If they were to be the light of the world and the salt of the earth, their righteousness must exceed that of the scribes and Pharisees. They must not try (like the casuists) to dodge the law's demands, or (like the hypocrites) to practise their piety before men, but realize that God sees in secret and looks on the heart. His disciples must be quite different from the Gentiles as well, in their love, their prayers and their ambition. They must love their enemies as well as their friends, renounce vain repetitions in prayer for an intelligent approach to their Father, and seek first, as the supreme good, not their own material necessities but the rule and the righteousness of God.

The people were astounded by Jesus' authority, for He taught neither like the scribes (who invariably quoted their authorities), nor even like the prophets (who spoke in the name of Jehovah), but with His own authority and in His own name, declaring 'truly, truly, I say to you'.

Moreover, He enforced His teaching with unforgettable parables, which illustrated the love of God for sinners (e.g. the Prodigal Son), the necessity of humble trust in God's mercy for salvation (e.g. the Pharisee and the Publican), the love which we ought to have for each other (e.g. the Good Samaritan), the way God's word is received and God's kingdom grows (e.g. the Sower and the Mustard Seed), the responsibility of disciples to develop and exercise their gifts (the Pounds and the

11

Talents), and the judgment of those who reject the gospel (e.g. the Wheat and the Tares).

Thirdly, He healed. He performed other miracles too, exhibiting His power over nature by stilling a storm on the lake, walking on water and multiplying loaves and fishes. But His commonest miracles were healing miracles, effected now by a touch of the hand, now by a bare word of command. From one point of view, the sufficient explanation of His healing ministry is His love, for He was moved to compassion by the sight of every form of suffering. But, in addition, His miracles were 'signs' both of God's kingdom and of His own deity. They signified that the Messiah's reign had begun, as the Scriptures had foretold. It was with this evidence that Jesus sought to reassure the doubts of John the Baptist in prison:

'Go and tell John what you have seen and heard: the blind receive their sight, the lame walk, lepers are cleansed, and the deaf hear, the dead are raised up, the poor have good news preached to them.'[20]

Similarly, the miracles were signs that the forces of evil were in full retreat before the advancing kingdom of God:

'But if it is by the finger of God that I cast out demons, then the kingdom of God has come upon you.'[21]

The miracles were also signs that Jesus was the Son of God, for each was an acted parable, dramatizing one of His divine claims. The feeding of the 5,000 set forth visibly His claim to be the bread of life, His healing of the man born blind His claim to be the light of the world, and His raising of the dead His claim to be the resurrection and the life.

In this threefold work of preaching, teaching and healing, Jesus also involved the Twelve. He seems to have chosen and called them early in this second year of His public ministry and, by surnaming them 'apostles', to have indicated the work to which they were being commissioned. I shall enlarge on this in a later chapter when we consider their unique authority. In human terms they were a motley and unpromising group, including four fishermen, one tax collector, at least one political zealot and another who proved to be a traitor. Yet He kept them with Him, training them by what they saw and heard, and sent them out two by two, endowed with His authority to preach and to heal like Him.

During the Galilean ministry the crowds kept growing. The whole countryside became tense with excitement and expectation:

'Great multitudes gathered to hear and to be healed of their infirmities.'[22]

The high tide of Jesus' popularity seems to have been reached at the time of the feeding of the 5,000. It took place just after the beheading of John the Baptist, an ugly omen of the turn of the tide. Since the 5,000 were all men, apart from women and children,[23] the total crowd must have been more than double that number. When the hunger of all had been satisfied as a result of the miraculous multiplication of five barley loaves and two pickled fish, the buzz of excitement reached fever pitch. The word began to go round the crowd 'This is surely the prophet who is to come into the world'. And as the rumour spread, the people made up their minds. They were determined to 'take Him by force to make Him king', that is, their national leader to liberate them from the dominion of Rome. But Jesus caught wind of it, and 'withdrew to the hills by Himself'.[24]

The Year of Adversity
Having returned to Capernaum on the other side of the lake, Jesus preached a sermon in the synagogue, using the

13

miracle of the loaves and fishes as His text. He had not come to be a political revolutionary. He was the bread of life, He said. Anyone who came to Him and believed in Him would never again be hungry or thirsty. And the bread He would give for the life of the world was His flesh. Immediately a dispute broke out among the Jews:

'How can this man give us His flesh to eat?'

Even His disciples found it a hard saying, and many of them 'drew back and no longer went about with him'.[25] The tide had turned.

So now Jesus again 'withdrew' and made more distant expeditions, beyond the boundaries of Galilee. He went to Tyre and Sidon in the north-west,[26] and to the Decapolis, a region south-east of the Lake.[27] Then later He travelled north again, this time to Caesarea Philippi, in the foothills of Mount Hermon.[28] Here a very important incident took place, which forms a kind of watershed in the gospel narrative. Jesus asked the Twelve who men were saying He was, and they gave Him the answers of popular speculation, that He was John the Baptist, Elijah or one of the prophets. But who did the Twelve say He was? Immediately Peter replied, 'You are the Christ'.

Our Lord's rejoinder comes as a shock to many readers, for He commanded them to tell no one about Him.[29] But the next verse explains the riddle:

'And He began to teach them that the Son of man must suffer many things, and be rejected by the elders and the chief priests and the scribes, and be killed, and after three days rise again. And He said this plainly.'[30]

Jesus' command to silence, repeated after several of the miracles, was due to His desire to keep His Messiahship secret so long as the people misunderstood its nature, as exemplified in their attempt to make Him a king by force.

But now that Peter had clearly confessed his faith, Jesus 'began' to teach the necessity of His sufferings and to do so 'plainly', i.e. openly. At first Peter could not accept this truth. But Jesus insisted on it and added that the same pattern of glory through suffering or life through death would be the experience of His followers as well.[31]

Six days later according to the synoptic evangelists Jesus took Peter, James and John with Him up a 'high mountain' (? Hermon) and was transfigured before them, His face and clothing becoming suffused with a bright light. It was a preview of His glory, the glory of His kingdom and of His resurrection body, the glory to which He would one day come through suffering.

When Jesus returned to Galilee it was for a largely private visit, since He was continuing to teach the disciples about His coming sufferings, and subsequent resurrection.[32] Soon after He began His journey south.[33] Indeed, 'He set His face to go to Jerusalem,[34] and on the way continued to emphasize the same things.[35] Luke supplies a number of details about this journey and its accompanying instruction, which the other evangelists do not record.[36] He tells us that Jesus referred to a baptism of suffering which He had to undergo and to His sense of constriction until it was accomplished.[37] Later He said:

> 'Behold, we are going up to Jerusalem, and everything that is written of the Son of man by the prophets will be accomplished'.[38]

The approach to Jerusalem was through Jericho, an oasis not far from where the Jordan flows into the Dead Sea. Here Jesus gave sight to blind Bartimaeus and salvation to Zacchaeus the shady tax-collector.[39] Then came the steep ascent along the desert road towards the holy city.

The impression conveyed by the Synoptic evangelists

15

is that Jesus went straight to Jerusalem and to the events of His last week. We know from John's gospel, however, that He spent about another six months in Judea, which included visits to Jerusalem for the Feast of Tabernacles in October and the Feast of Dedication in December.[40] Exactly where He was staying during this period is not clear, but sometimes it was in the wilderness of Judea and sometimes even the other side of the Jordan near the scene of His baptism.[41]

When He appeared in public for the festivals, His claims (attested by His signs) became ever clearer and bolder. He was the bestower of living water, He said, the light of the world (as evidenced in giving sight to a man born blind), the great 'I am' who lived eternally before Abraham, the good Shepherd who would lay down His life for His sheep and (when He raised Lazarus from death) both the resurrection and the life.[42] The Jewish leaders found these claims increasingly provocative, and it is several times recorded that they tried to arrest and kill Him.[43]

Already during His Galilean ministry, although the crowds gave Him tumultuous support, He did not escape the carping criticisms of the scribes and Pharisees. Mark assembles a series of four 'controversy stories' in which Jesus was accused first of blasphemy (for daring to forgive a man's sins), then of fraternizing with sinners, thirdly of religious laxity in failing to fast, and lastly of breaking the sabbath.[44] In defending Himself against these charges Jesus had only made matters worse in His critics' eyes by claiming to be the Son of man with authority to forgive, the physician who had come to heal sick sinners, the bridegroom in whose presence the wedding guests could not fast and the lord even of the sabbath.

As time passed He had gone further. He had condemned the Pharisees for their hypocrisy[45] and for exalting their man-made traditions above God's commandments,[46] and was later to rebuke the Sadducees for their ignorance of God's word and God's power.[47] Gradually the tension grew. The Jewish leaders were jealous of His reputation with the people, wounded by His exposure of their superficiality and put to shame by His own transparent integrity. It was only a matter of time before the final collision.

When Jesus approached Jerusalem for the last time and reached the point on the road round the Mount of Olives where the city came into view, He could not restrain His tears. He wept and said:

'Would that even today you knew the things that make for peace! But now they are hid from your eyes.'[48]

Nevertheless, despite what it seemed would be the city's certain rejection, He issued one last appeal. By a careful pre-arrangement He was able to ride into Jerusalem on a borrowed donkey, in order deliberately to fulfil the prophecy of Zechariah:

'Rejoice greatly, O daughter of Zion! Shout aloud, O daughter of Jerusalem! Lo, your king comes to you; triumphant and victorious is He, humble and riding on an ass, on a colt the foal of an ass.'[49]

The crowds that were accompanying Him were eager to acclaim Him. They cut branches from the trees and took off their cloaks to make a carpet for Him to ride over. They waved palm branches in the air and shouted their Hosannas. For this was His 'triumphal entry' into Jerusalem. But His triumph was not shared by the authorities, and it was short-lived. He antagonized them by cleansing the temple for the second time,[50] and during the next three days, from Monday to Wednesday, their hostility to Him became increasingly intense. They engaged Him in controversy, theological and political, although they could not fault Him in argument.[51] He for His part castigated the Pharisees for their religious pretence in a series of devastating 'woes',[52] and warned His apostles of the coming destruction of Jerusalem and of the opposition they must expect before His return would bring history to its end.[53]

The Death and Resurrection of Jesus

The Thursday of this last week was by one reckoning the eve of the Passover and by another the Passover itself. Jesus knew that His 'hour', which He had repeatedly said was 'not yet', had at last come. It was to be an hour of unparalleled suffering, and yet also the hour of His 'glorification' by which He would be most fully revealed and the salvation even of the Gentiles would be accomplished.[54]

He spent His final hours of liberty privately with the Twelve in a furnished, first-floor room lent Him by a friend. Here they ate the Passover meal together. During supper He performed a slave's work, which evidently none of them had been willing to do, for He went round washing their feet. He told them that they must humble themselves and love one another like that. During and after supper He also gave them bread and wine as emblems of His body and blood which were to be offered for their salvation, and commanded them to eat and drink in His memory. Then He fortified them by profound instruction about the new and intimate relationship with Him which the coming Holy Spirit would make possible, and He prayed for them that the Father would keep them what they were, a distinct people, who no longer belonged to the world but were to continue living in it as His representatives.

It must have been late when they left the upper room, walked through the deserted city streets, crossed the Kidron valley and began to climb the Mount of Olives.

In the garden of Gethsemane Jesus prayed with an agony of desire that He might be spared having to drink 'this cup', an Old Testament symbol of God's wrath upon sin. But he ended each prayer with a fresh surrender of His will, and emerged with a quiet, unshakeable resolve to drink it. At that very moment the temple soldiers arrived to arrest Him, carrying torches and weapons, and Judas betrayed Him to them.

There now followed a gruelling series (that night and the following morning) of six separate trials, three in Jewish courts, one before Herod and two before Pontius Pilate. When false witnesses accused Him, Jesus was silent, but when the high priest challenged Him whether He was 'the Christ, the Son of God', He boldly acknowledged that He was and was immediately condemned to death for blasphemy. This travesty of justice was made the more bitter for Him by the brutality of those who struck Him and spat in His face, and by the cowardly denials of Peter in the courtyard outside.

Since by Roman law the Jews were not permitted to carry out the death sentence, it was necessary for them to get it ratified by the procurator. Pontius Pilate is known to have been an efficient administrator, but ruthless. He quickly saw through the political charge of which the Jews accused Jesus, namely that He had forbidden the payment of tribute to Caesar and had made claims to be a king Himself. A few questions about Jesus' kingship satisfied him that the prisoner was no revolutionary agitator. But Pilate was a man ruled more by expediency than by principle. He wanted both to release Jesus and to satisfy the Jews simultaneously. So he tried various compromise arrangements. Would they be content if Jesus received a scourging, or a trial by Herod or the customary Passover clemency? But the Jews would not allow him to escape a decision. When they hinted that if Pilate released Jesus he would forfeit Caesar's favour, his mind was made up. He washed his hands publicly in feigned innocence and handed Jesus over to them to be mocked, flogged and crucified.

Crucifixion was a horrible form of execution. To the Romans it was a shameful thing; they reserved it for slaves and the worst criminals. It was a sadistic kind of torture too, for it deliberately prolonged the pain and postponed death sometimes even for days.

How Jesus viewed and endured His ordeal is shown by the seven 'words' which He spoke from the cross. The first three indicate that He was able so to forget His own suffering as to concern Himself entirely with the welfare of others. He prayed that His tormentors might be forgiven; He commended His mother to John's care, and John to His mother's; and He assured the penitent brigand who was being crucified at His side that he would be with Him that very day in paradise.[55] After this Jesus seems to have been silent for several hours, while a strange darkness overshadowed the land. Then he uttered four cries, perhaps in quick succession, which give us some idea of the nature and purpose of His sufferings.[56] First, 'I thirst', betraying His physical anguish. Then 'My God, My God, why hast thou forsaken Me?' This cry of dereliction was framed as a question not because He did not know the answer, but because He was quoting Psalm 22.1. And He quoted it (as He always quoted Scripture) because He believed He was fulfilling it. The Godforsakenness which He experienced was the divine judgment which our sins deserved. He was drinking the 'cup' of God's wrath. Almost immediately came a loud cry of triumph, the single word 'Finished', expressing His accomplishment of the sin-bearing work He had come to do. Finally, He commended His spirit to the Father, to show that His death was a voluntary, self-determined act:

'Father, into Thy hands I commit My spirit'[57]

About thirty-six hours later God raised Him from the dead, as a decisive proof that He had not died in vain. At first light of dawn on Easter Day, Mary Magdalene and some other women came to Joseph of Arimathea's tomb, in order to complete the burial rites which the onset of the sabbath had interrupted. But they found that the stone had been rolled aside from the mouth of the tomb and that the tomb itself was empty. Hearing the news, Peter and John raced to the sepulchre. Looking in, they discovered not only that the Lord's body had gone, but that His grave-clothes were still there, lying in an undisturbed condition. It was clear circumstantial evidence that the body had not been touched by human hands but raised from death by God. They 'saw and believed'.

Then the risen Lord began to appear. First individually to Mary Magdalene and to Peter. Then to two disciples on the road from Jerusalem to Emmaus. Then to the apostles the same evening, and again the following Sunday when Thomas (absent the previous week) was with them. Next, when they had returned to Galilee, He appeared to them there also, both on a mountain and on the lakeshore. At every appearance He gave them evidence that it was He Himself, the same person as before His death, though now marvellously changed, and He commissioned them to go into the whole world and to make all nations His disciples.

These appearances continued for forty days. The last one took place on the Mount of Olives. Having promised them power to be His witnesses once the Holy Spirit had come upon them, and having blessed them, He was 'taken up . . . into heaven'. There is no need to doubt the literal nature of His ascension, so long as we realize its purpose. It was not necessary as a mode of departure, for 'going to the Father' did not involve a journey in space and presumably He could simply have vanished as on previous occasions. The reason He ascended before their eyes was rather to show them that this departure was final. He had now gone for good, or at least until His coming in glory. So they returned to Jerusalem with great joy and waited—not for Jesus to make another resurrection appearance, but for the Holy Spirit to come in power, as had been promised.

The Infant Church

The disciples had only ten days to wait. Then suddenly, while they were praying together for the promise to be fulfilled, it happened. Accompanied by the noise of wind and the appearance of fiery flames, the Holy Spirit came and filled them all. It was the culminating event of Christ's saving career, for, as Peter explained in his sermon that same morning, it was Jesus Christ who brought the significance of His birth, death, resurrection and ascension to its climax by pouring out His Spirit from heaven.

Pentecost must also be understood as a fundamentally missionary event. The miracle of the foreign languages which the disciples spoke symbolized the international Christian community which was about to be brought to birth by the gospel.

Three thousand people were converted, baptized and added to the church that day:

> 'And they devoted themselves to the apostles' teaching and fellowship, to the breaking of bread and the prayers'[58]

One marvels at the clarity and forcefulness of the early preaching of the apostles. Luke gives us four sample sermons by Peter—on the Day of Pentecost, after the healing of the cripple outside the temple's Beautiful

Gate, before the Jewish Council and to the household of Cornelius.[59] Although of course he supplies only a précis of each, it is enough to show the content and pattern of Peter's proclamation.

Peter preached Jesus Christ, His life, death and resurrection. During His life He was divinely attested by miracles. His death was due both to the purpose of God and to the wickedness of men.[60] Though men denied and killed Him, God vindicated Him by raising Him from the dead. And now He is exalted as Lord, Christ, Saviour and Judge. Moreover, all this is doubly confirmed by the testimony of Old Testament Scripture and of the apostolic eye-witnesses. Therefore, let them repent of their sin, believe in the name of Jesus Christ and be baptized, for then they will receive the blessing promised to Abraham's seed, namely the forgiveness of sins and the gift of the Spirit.

It must not be imagined, however, that the infant church had no problems. No sooner had Jesus Christ through His Spirit launched His offensive to conquer the world than the devil mounted a powerful counter-attack. His strategy was threefold.

First, he tried the crude weapon of persecution.[61] When Peter and John started 'teaching the people and proclaiming in Jesus the resurrection of the dead',[62] they were arrested and brought to trial before the Sanhedrin. Here they witnessed to Jesus with wonderful boldness, declaring Him to be the only Saviour. The council was deeply impressed, knowing them to be uneducated men, but forbade them to 'speak or teach at all in the name of Jesus'. Peter and John replied that they must obey God not men, and that in any case they simply could not help speaking of what they had seen and heard. Then, after they had been further threatened, they were let go. The apostles went straight to their Christian friends and together they prayed to the sovereign Lord of nature

23

and of history not for their safety and protection, but that they might be given courage to go on speaking His word. So the preaching went on. They were again arrested, and now imprisoned, but an angel of the Lord released them and told them to go and preach the gospel in the sacred precincts of the temple itself. Once more they were arrested and brought to trial, but this time the Jewish Council, cautioned by the Pharisee Gamaliel that they might be found opposing God, did no more than beat them and repeat their injunction not to speak in the name of Jesus. The reaction of the apostles?

'They left the presence of the council, rejoicing that they were counted worthy to suffer dishonour for the name. And every day in the temple and at home they did not cease teaching and preaching Jesus as the Christ'[63]

The other weapons which the devil wielded against the church were more subtle. Unable to crush it by external pressure, he tried to undermine it from within.

24

The generosity of the early Christians had led many of them to sell their lands and bring the proceeds to the apostles for the relief of those in need. A married couple called Ananias and Sapphira decided to do the same, but then to keep back part of the money for themselves while pretending to surrender it all. Their property was entirely at their own disposal both before and after the sale, as Peter later made clear. They were under no obligation to give any of it away. Their sin was that they wanted the credit for giving everything, without the cost. If they had succeeded in their intrigue, hypocrisy would have begun to seep into the Christian community. Peter detected their lie, however, and they paid for their duplicity with their lives.[64]

The third Satanic weapon was the most indirect. It was to preoccupy the apostles with social administration (to be precise, the care of Christian widows) and so divert them from the teaching role to which God had called them. But the apostles were alert to this danger. So they delegated the task. They instructed the body of the disciples to choose seven 'deacons' (as they are usually called) to take over the church's welfare work, so that they could devote themselves to their God-given priority, namely 'to prayer and to the ministry of the word'.[65]

When the devil's initial three-pronged counter-offensive had failed, Luke was able to write:

'And the word of God increased; and the number of the disciples multiplied greatly in Jerusalem.'[66]

One of the seven was Stephen, a Christian man full of grace, faith, wisdom and power. Accused of speaking against the law of Moses and the temple, he was brought before the Council. His defence, recorded in Acts 7, is a masterly narrative of God's dealings with Israel, designed to demonstrate that God is tied to no place or building but only to His people whose God He is. He

25

ended his speech by accusing his accusers. They were stiff-necked, he said, always resistant to the Holy Spirit, and now guilty of murdering the Christ. At this they rushed on him, threw him out of the city and stoned him to death.

But in the providence of God the death of the first Christian martyr helped rather than hindered the spread of the gospel. For the persecution of Christians which followed it scattered them throughout Judea and Samaria, and wherever they went they preached the word.[67] Among them was Philip, who was another of the seven 'deacons'. He was given conspicuous success in evangelizing Samaritans, who for centuries had been repudiated by the Jews. So the apostles (who had stayed behind in Jerusalem) sent Peter and John to investigate and endorse what had happened, thus avoiding a continuance within the church of the Jewish-Samaritan schism. Philip also explained the good news of Christ crucified to an Ethiopian state official who was on his way back home from Jerusalem.[68]

This outreach to Samaria and Ethiopia was only the prelude to the Gentile mission which soon began. Luke introduces it in *Acts* with two significant conversions, of Saul of Tarsus and (through Peter's witness) of the Roman centurion Cornelius. These events indicate the vital part played by the great apostles Paul and Peter in opening the gates of the church to Gentiles.

Saul of Tarsus is first mentioned as the man who minded the clothing of those who were stoning Stephen. It is conjectured that he never forgot the courage and love of this Christian martyr who prayed for the forgiveness of his enemies. But he continued to stifle the voice of conscience and savagely to persecute the church, until that memorable day (described no fewer than three times in *Acts*) when Jesus Christ appeared to him on the road to Damascus and (as he was later to put it) 'apprehended' him. After reaching Damascus he learned from Ananias that he had been called to be an apostle as well as a disciple, and to be Christ's chosen instrument to carry His name before Gentiles as well as Jews.[69] His conversion must have taken place between three and five years only after the crucifixion.

Almost two complete chapters of *Acts* are devoted to the story of Cornelius' conversion, so important an event did Luke consider it.[70] For Cornelius, although a 'godfearer' on the fringe of the synagogue, was still a Gentile outsider. It took a special vision to convince Peter that he should enter Cornelius' house and preach the gospel to him, and it took a special repetition of Pentecost (as I think we may describe it) to convince him that God now made no distinction between Jews and Gentiles but granted His cleansing and His Spirit to all believers without discrimination.[71] It was an immense leap forward.

Some of those who left Jerusalem after Stephen's martyrdom travelled north to Antioch, which was the capital of Syria and the third most renowned city in the Empire. They preached the Lord Jesus to the Greeks, and a great number believed. Hearing about this, the Jerusalem church sent Barnabas to Antioch, and he in his turn fetched Paul to help him. For a whole year these two men taught the converts. Here (in Antioch) the first Gentile church was established, for the first time the disciples were called Christians, and the first missionary expedition was launched.[72] The date was now about 47 A.D.

The First Missionary Journey

The missionaries chosen, set apart by the church in obedience to the Spirit's leading, were Barnabas and Paul, who then invited Mark (Barnabas' cousin) to accompany them. They sailed to Cyprus, Barnabas' home country, and then north-west to land on Asian soil at Perga in Pamphylia. By this time Mark had had enough and returned to Jerusalem. Perhaps he was scared of the swamps of Pamphylia where (conjecturally) Paul caught malaria which damaged his eyesight. At all events, when they had climbed the plateau and reached Galatia, Paul seems to have had some disfiguring eye disease.[73] The first Galatian city he visited was Pisidian Antioch, where he preached in the synagogue and many Jews were converted. But when the unbelieving Jews contradicted Paul's message, he took a bold step (which in the future he would often repeat) and turned to the Gentiles. Driven out of the city by opposition, Paul and Barnabas moved on to three more Galatian towns, Iconium, Lystra (where pagans nearly worshipped them as gods and Jews stoned Paul as a blasphemer) and Derbe. Then, retracing their steps, they strengthened the new converts and in every church appointed elders to care for them.[74]

Back in Antioch they gathered the church together and reported what God had done, especially 'how He had opened a door of faith to the Gentiles'.[75] But the church's rejoicing soon gave place to controversy, for there arrived in Antioch from Jerusalem a group of so-called 'Judaizers', who started teaching that unless Gentile converts were circumcised and kept the law of Moses they could not be saved.[76] Paul engaged them in a vigorous debate. And when even Peter, in a temporary lapse due to fear rather than conviction, withdrew from fellowship with Gentile Christians, Paul had to rebuke him publicly.[77]

It appears that the insidious influence of the Judaizers had penetrated even to the Galatian churches. This prompted Paul to write the first of his many letters. In his *Letter to the Galatians* he defended his apostolic authority as derived from Christ, assured them that there

28

was no discord between him and the Jerusalem apostles, rejected the Judaizers' gospel as being no gospel at all, emphasized that salvation is by God's grace alone through faith alone without the addition of circumcision or the works of the law or anything else, and begged his Galatian readers to stand fast in their Christian liberty.

The church of Antioch decided to send Paul and Barnabas to Jerusalem to settle the issue which had been raised by the Judaizers, and this led to 'the Council of Jerusalem' (described in Acts 15) in about 49 or 50 A.D. After much debate Peter (who by now had recovered from his lapse) recounted the conversion of Cornelius. Then Paul and Barnabas told what God had done through their ministry among the Gentiles. Finally James, the Lord's brother, clinched the argument from Old Testament Scripture. Gentile converts, he concluded, did not need to be circumcised in order to be saved. Nevertheless, in order to respect the scruples of weak Jewish consciences and so promote Gentile-Jewish fellowship within the church, they were to be asked voluntarily to follow certain Jewish food and marriage regulations.[78]

It is almost certainly to this James that we owe the New Testament *Letter of James*. It may have been written about this time. It is evidently a Jewish Christian homily, whose emphasis is that a true, living and saving faith will be evidenced by a life of brotherly love, self-control and devotion to God.

The Second Missionary Journey

Armed with a letter from the Jerusalem apostles and elders, containing the decisions of the Council, Paul set out on his second missionary journey, this time accompanied by Silas.[79] They revisited the Galatian churches, delivering the Council's decree. At Lystra Paul invited Timothy to accompany them. Because he had a Gentile father, Paul even circumcized him out of deference to local Jews, for now that the principle of salvation by grace alone had been established he was ready to make such a policy concession.[80]

Forbidden by the Holy Spirit (in ways not explained) to journey either south-west towards Ephesus or due north into Bithynia, Paul and his companions were shut up to going in a north-westerly direction and so arrived at Troas on the Aegean coast. Here Paul had a dream in which a Greek begged him to go over to Macedonia and help them. He and his friends interpreted the vision as a call from God to take the gospel into Europe. And Luke, the author of *Acts*, by using the pronoun 'we' for the first time in his narrative, quietly indicates that he sailed with them.

Macedonia was the northern province of Greece, and the missionary team preached the gospel in three of its principal towns—Philippi (where Paul and Silas spent a memorable night in prison, with their feet in the stocks), Thessalonica (where during a three-week mission a great many believed) and Beroea. Paul then moved on to Achaia, the southern province of Greece, visiting its two chief cities, Athens and Corinth.

There is something very moving about the picture of Paul in Athens, the Christian apostle alone amid the glories of ancient Greece. As he walked through the city it was not the beauty which struck him, however, but the idolatry. This stirred him deeply, and first in the synagogue with the Jews, then in the market place with passers-by, and finally before the famous Council of the Areopagus with the Stoic and Epicurean philosophers, he faithfully preached Jesus, the resurrection and the judgment to come.

Timothy joined him while he was in Athens, but Paul was so concerned to discover how the Thessalonian church was faring under persecution that he sent him off

Paul's Missionary Journeys

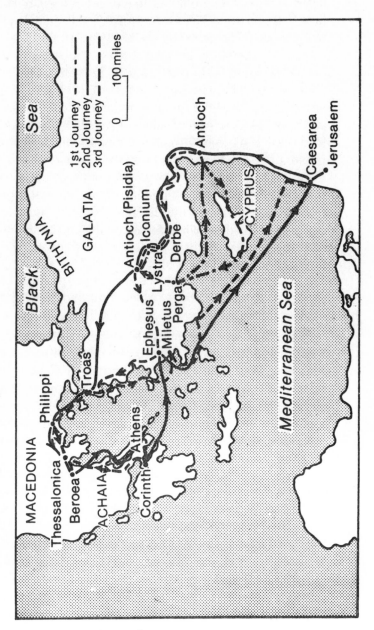

31

again at once to find out and to encourage them to stand firm.[81] By the time Timothy returned, Paul had moved on to Corinth.[82] The good news he brought was the occasion of his *First Letter to the Thessalonians*, with *the Second Letter* following it soon afterwards. In these letters Paul rejoices over the Thessalonians' faith, love and steadfastness, and over the example which they are setting to all the believers in Macedonia and Achaia.[83] He goes on to defend his personal integrity against his Jewish detractors.[84] Then he exhorts his readers to earn their own living and not to give up work on the false supposition that the Lord's return is imminent; to take courage in their bereavement because the living will not take precedence over the dead when Jesus comes; and to live lives of sexual purity. Perhaps he has these three categories in his mind when he writes:

'Admonish the idle, encourage the fainthearted, help the weak.'[85]

Paul stayed in Corinth for the best part of two years. He followed his normal custom of bearing witness to the Jews first, and won a notable convert in Crispus, the ruler of the synagogue. But when the Jews opposed and abused him, he again turned to the Gentiles and received support in his policy from an unexpected quarter, the proconsul of Achaia called Gallio. It was a truly wonderful triumph of God's grace that a Jewish-Gentile church should arise in such a cesspool of vice as Corinth was.

The Third Missionary Journey

Paul's voyage back to Antioch was interrupted by a brief visit to Ephesus, the principal city of the Roman province of Asia. He must have been so impressed by its strategic importance, that he went almost straight there at the beginning of his third missionary journey.[86] After three months' preaching in the synagogue he broke fresh ground in evangelistic method. He hired 'the hall of Tyrannus', presumably a secular school or lecture hall, and here every day for two years, according to some manuscripts 'from the fifth hour to the tenth' (i.e. from 11 a.m. to 4 p m.), argued the gospel. Assuming that he worked a six-day week, this represents 3,120 hours of gospel argument. It is not surprising that as a result 'all the residents of Asia heard the word of the Lord'.[87]

While he was in Ephesus, the Corinthian church gave him much cause for anxiety on both doctrinal and moral grounds. His first letter to them (mentioned in 1 Cor. 5.9) has been lost. However, on receiving disquieting news from some Corinthian travellers, who also brought with them a number of questions from the church, Paul wrote them a second letter which is our *First Corinthians*. In it he is able to thank God for the gifts with which Christ has enriched them,[88] but he deplores the factions into which the church has been split and their false view of the ministry which lies behind the factions.[89] He also expresses indignant horror at the immorality and litigation which they are tolerating among their members,[90] and at the irregularities they are permitting in public worship.[91] In answer to their questions he writes about marriage,[92] about the eating of food offered to idols,[93] and about the use and abuse of spiritual gifts.[94] He then summarizes his gospel and emphasizes particularly the resurrection of Christ and of Christians.[95]

This letter evidently failed to have its desired effect, for Paul decided to visit Corinth personally. He later referred to this as a 'painful visit',[96] because apparently one of the church leaders openly defied his authority. So serious was this challenge that on leaving Paul wrote them yet another letter (usually referred to as the 'severe letter'), insisting that the offender be punished. This letter also seems to have been lost, unless (as some scholars

33

believe) it has somehow found its way into 2 Corinthians 10–13. At all events, the severe letter was heeded and the offender was duly disciplined. Paul was overjoyed to hear from Titus of their loyalty[97] and immediately wrote to them again.

In this letter, our *Second Corinthians*, he begs them now to 'forgive and comfort' the rebel, who has received a sufficient punishment.[98] He goes on to write of the glory, problems and responsibilities of the Christian ministry,[99] devotes two chapters to the appeal that he has launched to the churches of Macedonia and Achaia to raise money for the impoverished church of Judea,[100] and concludes with a lengthy defence of his apostolic authority.[101]

He mentioned in this letter his intention to pay them a third visit,[102] which eventually came to pass. Ephesus boasted a magnificent temple to the goddess Artemis (or Diana), which was one of the seven wonders of the world. As the number of Ephesian converts from idolatry grew, the silversmiths saw a strong threat to their trade in shrines or souvenirs of the goddess.[103] A serious riot ensued, and Paul left the city for Macedonia and then Achaia.[104]

It appears that the apostle stayed about three months in Corinth in the home of Gaius, and that from here he wrote his great *Letter to the Romans*.[105] In it he tells the Christians in Rome how eager he is not only to visit and encourage them, but also to preach the gospel in the world's capital city[106] and then to travel on into Spain.[107] So he takes the opportunity to unfold at length this gospel which is committed to him and to which he is committed. He describes the terrible degradation of mankind, and argues that there is no distinction between Jew and Gentile in the fact of their sin and guilt.[108] Neither is there any distinction between them regarding the offer of salvation:

'For there is no distinction between Jew and Greek;
the same Lord is Lord of all and bestows His riches
upon all who call upon Him.'[109]

This salvation is a free gift offered by God's grace,
grounded upon Christ's death and—as the Old Testament itself makes plain—received by man's faith not
earned by his works.[110] Faith not only justifies the
sinner, but unites him to Christ. And 'in Christ', that is,
joined to Christ by faith (invisibly) and by baptism
(visibly), the Christian begins an altogether new life of
freedom. He is free from the dominion of sin through
slavery to God,[111] free from the bondage of the law
through the indwelling Spirit,[112] and free from all fear
of evil, whether in life or in death, through the assurance
of being God's son for ever.[113]

Next Paul wrestles with a problem which troubled him
deeply: How is it that the Jews, God's specially privileged
people, have not accepted Jesus as their Messiah? It is
certainly not that God's word of promise has failed.
The strange phenomenon of their unbelief can be understood in the light partly of the mysterious process of
God's election,[114] partly of their own rebellion as 'a
disobedient and contrary people',[115] and partly of a
broad historical perspective that one day 'the fulness' of
Jews as well as Gentiles will come in and 'so all Israel
will be saved'.[116]

After this digression Paul comes back to the life of
practical holiness which, because of 'the mercies of God',
all His people should lead—in mutual service,[117] in
conscientious citizenship,[118] and in the brotherly love
which accepts even the weak brother who has an over-
scrupulous conscience.[119]

Leaving Corinth, Paul and his companions began their
long journey to Jerusalem,[120] taking with them the now
completed collection for the Judean church. Among the
ports at which they called were Troas (where Paul's

sermon lasted till midnight and their fellowship till daybreak!) and Miletus (where Paul gave a moving address to the elders of the Ephesian church).

Paul's Arrest and Journey to Rome

When at last they reached their destination, they had not been in Jerusalem a week before some Asian Jews started maliciously alleging that Paul had undermined Moses' law by his teaching and defiled the temple by bringing Greeks into it. A riot broke out, and Paul was rescued from being lynched by the prompt action of the military tribune.[121]

During the next two years and more the apostle was held a prisoner. During the same period Luke was at liberty in Palestine, no doubt gathering material for his Gospel and the *Acts*. Paul had to undergo a series of trials in Jerusalem and Caesarea before the Sanhedrin,[122] before the procurator Felix,[123] before his successor Festus,[124] and before King Agrippa and his wife Bernice.[125] But since as a Roman citizen he had exercised his right to appeal to Caesar, he was eventually sent to Rome for trial.

The long and perilous sea voyage included the exciting escape from shipwreck on the island of Malta, which Luke tells with graphic detail,[126] and at last Paul reached the Rome of his dreams. The Christians welcomed him, and the Jews came to visit him and hear the gospel from his lips.

Luke has now traced the spread of the gospel from Jerusalem the capital of Jewry to Rome the capital of the world. He ends his narrative with a picture of his hero, the apostle Paul, who although under house arrest was still an indefatigable evangelist:

'he . . . welcomed all who came to him, preaching the

36

kingdom of God and teaching about the Lord Jesus Christ quite openly and unhindered.'[127]

It was not only by spoken witness, however, that the apostle exploited his two years' imprisonment in Rome. He also spent time writing to various churches, and the so-called 'prison epistles' which belong to this period are the letters to the *Ephesians* (probably a circular letter to Asian churches of that region), to the *Colossians*, to *Philemon* (a personal letter instructing him to receive back as a brother his runaway slave, now converted) and to the *Philippians* (though some think this letter was written earlier from a supposed imprisonment in Ephesus). It is not easy to give a resumé of the message of these letters, for each was occasioned by a different local situation. Yet if there is one truth which stands out in them all, it is the greatness of Jesus Christ. The very fulness of God, Paul writes, was pleased both to dwell in Him and to work through Him, on the one hand creating the universe and on the other reconciling all things to Himself. He has now been exalted to God's right hand, far above all principalities and powers, and has been given the pre-eminent name, so that every knee should bow to Him and every tongue confess Him Lord. This cosmic Christ is also the head of the church, whose members are called to be what they are, a holy, united and victorious people.

The supremacy of Christ is also the theme of a very different New Testament book, the *Letter to the Hebrews*. Both its author and its destination are unknown, for neither is named in it. But its purpose is to prevent certain Jewish Christians from lapsing into Judaism, by emphasizing the finality of Jesus Christ. In Him all priesthood and sacrifice have been fulfilled, and by Him an eternal redemption has been won.

37

Since Luke concludes the *Acts* with Paul's arrival and ministry in Rome, we are left somewhat in the dark about the following years. But it seems certain that Paul was released from custody (as he expected) and that he resumed his travels for another year or two. He visited Crete and left Titus there.[128] Soon afterwards he wrote him his *Letter to Titus* to remind him of his responsibilities. He must appoint suitable elders in every town who would be able to combat false teaching. He himself should also be a teacher and emphasize the kind of Christian conduct which is appropriate in those who have embraced 'the sound doctrine' of the gospel of salvation.

Paul then went on to Ephesus, where he left Timothy for similar reasons.[129] In his *First Letter to Timothy* he gives him instructions how to deal with false teachers, conduct public worship, select candidates for the pastorate, exercise his own ministry in such a way that his comparative youth will not be despised, arrange for the care of Christian widows, give balanced advice about money and behave like a man of God. It is a truly 'pastoral epistle' (as the letters to Timothy and Titus are usually known), containing much practical wisdom for church leaders today.

Then Paul journeyed on, perhaps to Colosse,[130] then to Macedonia[131] and then across Greece to Nicopolis,[132] the capital of Epirus on the Adriatic. Perhaps it was his intention when winter ended to sail from there for Spain. Whether he succeeded we may never know, though early tradition says he did. In any case, at some point he was re-arrested. It may have been at Troas, so that he had to leave his personal possessions behind, including a cloak and some books and parchments.[133] This time his prison in Rome was not the comparative liberty of a house arrest, but probably a dismal underground dungeon.

From such an imprisonment he wrote his *Second Letter to Timothy*. He felt keenly his loneliness, for only Luke was with him. He begged Timothy to come and visit him soon, and in any case before the winter would make sailing impossible. But his great concern was not for himself but for the gospel, the precious 'deposit' which he had committed to Timothy and which Timothy must now hand on to faithful men who would pass it to others also. Timothy must persevere in it himself and guard it from every falsification. He must be prepared, if need be, to suffer for it. Above all, he must preach it urgently and faithfully. Paul himself had preached the gospel fully during the first hearing of his case, so that 'all the Gentiles', crowded into the place of his trial, had heard it.[134] It was a fitting conclusion to his life of testimony. Now at last he could say:

> 'I have fought the good fight, I have finished the race, I have kept the faith. Henceforth there is laid up for me the crown of righteousness, which the Lord, the righteous judge, will award to me on that Day. . . .'[135]

Tradition says that Paul was beheaded (as a Roman citizen would have been) on the Ostian Way. His execution was probably a part of the persecution which broke out in Rome in A.D. 64 when Nero tried to deflect responsibility for the great fire from himself to the Christians.

This same Neronian persecution forms the background to the *First Letter of Peter*. He wrote it from Rome[136] and addressed it to Christians in the northern parts of Asia Minor to whom, he anticipated, the persecution was about to spread. He calls it a 'fiery ordeal'.[137] They are not to be surprised by it as something strange, nor to be afraid, but rather to rejoice at their privilege of sharing Christ's sufferings.[138] Indeed, the patient endurance of undeserved suffering is an inescapable part of the Christian calling, since Christians are followers of Christ, the suffering servant of the Lord.[139] The apostle Peter had soon to put his own instruction into practice, for he too (like Paul) was executed during the Neronian persecution, according to tradition by being crucified upside down.

The New Testament ends as *The Acts* begins, namely with Satanic attacks on the church from within and from without. The three *Letters of John*, written some time after the martyrdoms of Paul and Peter, warn the churches of the neighbourhood of Ephesus of a particular kind of Gnosticism. The heretics concerned denied that Jesus was 'the Christ come in the flesh', claimed to enjoy an experience of God without having to be righteous, and made arrogant pretensions to a superior enlightenment which led them to despise the unenlightened. Over against them John emphasized the truth of the divine-human person of Christ, the necessity of moral obedience and the centrality of love. The *Second Letter of Peter* and *the Letter of Jude* were also written to counter the promoters of 'anti-nomianism', false teachers who degraded Christian liberty into licence.[140] God's judgment would fall upon them.

The background to *the Book of Revelation* is probably the more severe and widespread persecution which was initiated by the Emperor Domitian (A.D. 81–96). Because of his faithful testimony John finds himself exiled to the little island of Patmos, some miles off shore from Ephesus.[141] Here he is given an 'apocalypse' or unveiling. In a sense the books of *Acts* and of *Revelation* are complementary. For *Acts* portrays the beginning of the church's mission and persecution as they appeared on the stage of history, whereas *Revelation* enables us to peep behind the scenes and glimpse the unseen spiritual battle which is raging between Christ and Satan.

John's visions are full of weird symbolism. Satan appears as 'a great red dragon with seven heads and ten horns', who declares war on the church. His three allies are two fearful monsters and a gaudy prostitute. The 'beast rising out of the sea' represents the persecuting power of the state, the second 'beast which rose out of the earth' (also called 'the false prophet') represents the cult of emperor-worship and indeed all erroneous teaching, while 'the great harlot' clothed in scarlet and decked with jewels, whose name is 'Babylon', represents the sinful enticements of worldliness. Persecution, error and evil are still the three major weapons which the devil wields in his fight against the church. But he will not prevail against it.

For *the Book of Revelation* is supremely a revelation of Jesus Christ as the Lamb who fights and conquers the Dragon. He is seen in other guises too, now patrolling and supervising His church, now sharing the Father's throne, now riding forth on a white horse as King of kings and Lord of lords to judge the nations, now coming as the Bridegroom to claim His bride. The whole book is a *sursum corda*, summoning hard-pressed Christian people to lift up their hearts and take courage. For Christ Jesus has died to ransom His people for God out of every nation. He is reigning now from His heavenly throne. And He is coming soon to judge and to save.

The church's prayer, with which the Bible ends, is 'Come, Lord Jesus.' And the church's assurance throughout its tribulation is that, until He comes, 'the grace of the Lord Jesus Christ' is sufficient to sustain all His people.[142]

Some Dates to Remember

The chronology of the New Testament period is difficult to determine with precision, although some dates are known. In areas of uncertainty, however, scholars differ from one another only by a year or two. One of the more commonly accepted reconstructions of events is given below.

B.C.

c. 5   The birth of Jesus

4   The death of Herod the Great

A.D.

30   The death, resurrection and ascension of Jesus. Pentecost.

c. 33   The conversion of Saul of Tarsus

44   The death of Herod Agrippa I (Acts 12.20–23)

c. 47, 48 The first missionary journey (Acts 13, 14)

c. 49   The Council of Jerusalem (Acts 15)

c. 49–52 The second missionary journey (Acts 16.1– 18.22)

c. 52–56 The third missionary journey (Acts 18.23– 21.17)

c. 57   Paul's arrest in Jerusalem (Acts 21.27–23.30)

c. 57–59 Paul's imprisonment in Caesarea (Acts 23.31– 26.32)

c. 60, 61 Paul under house arrest in Rome (Acts 28.14– 31)

c. 62–64 Paul at liberty again

64   The fire of Rome. Nero's persecution of Christians

c. 65   The martyrdom of Paul

70   The destruction of Jerusalem by Titus

81–96 The reign of the emperor Domitian. Widespread persecution

c. 100 The death of the apostle John

For Further Reading

The Message of the New Testament by F. F. Bruce (Paternoster 1972, 120 pages). The Rylands Professor of Biblical Criticism and Exegesis in the University of Manchester devotes one chapter to each book or group of books, beginning with Mark, the earliest Gospel, and concluding with the Johannine Epistles and Gospel. Aimed at the non-specialist, it offers a comprehensive view rather than a minute scrutiny.

The Life and Teaching of Jesus Christ by James S. Stewart (The Church of Scotland Committee on Youth. 1933. Second edition 1957, 209 pages). Written as part of the Church of Scotland's four years' course for Bible classes, this book by a distinguished theologian-preacher is both instructive and readable. After introductory chapters on 'The Gospel Records' and 'The Fulness of the Time' the story of Christ's life is unfolded stage by stage, and is interspersed with summaries of His teaching on particular subjects.

Beginning in Bible Archaeology by Howard F. Voo (Moody Press 1973, 112 pages). A complementary volume to Edwin Yamauchi's book (p.110) which begins with the method of approach to modern archaeology and then proceeds to consider the contribution which it makes to an understanding of the social life and history of biblical times. The result is a powerful apologetic for the trustworthiness of Scripture. There is a good bibliography to encourage further reading.

New Testament Times by Merrill C. Tenney (IVF 1965, 396 pages). A well-documented standard work of reference by the former Dean of the Graduate School, Wheaton College, Illinois. The historical, political, cultural and religious background is first thoroughly portrayed. The author then takes us systematically through the New Testament, making judicious and enlightening comments on the way. Copiously enriched by photographs, maps and charts. A mine of information.

NOTES

1 Acts 1.1
2 Lk. 1.1–4
3 Jn. 14.25, 26
4 1 Pet. 5.13 cf. Acts 12.11, 12
5 Mt. 9.9
6 Eusebius' *Ecclesiastical History* III.39.16
7 Jn. 20.30, 31
8 Jn. 1.1–14
9 Lk. 1.35
10 John mentions three Passovers in his narrative (2.13; 6.4 and 11.55)
11 Mt. 3 cf. Ps. 2.7 and Is. 42.1
12 Jn. 2.1–11
13 Jn. 2.19
14 The story of Nicodemus is recorded in Jn. 3.1 ff. and of the woman of Samaria in Jn. 4.4 ff.
15 Jn. 3.22–30
16 Jn. 3.24; 4.1–3; Mk. 1.14
17 Lk. 4.18, 19
18 Mt. 4.23 cf. 9.35
19 Mk. 1.14, 15
20 Lk. 7.22
21 Lk. 11.20
22 Lk. 5.15
23 Mt. 14.21
24 Jn. 6.14, 15
25 Jn. 6.52, 66
26 Mk. 7.24
27 Mk. 7.31
28 Mk. 8.27
29 Mk. 8.30
30 Mk. 8.31, 32
31 Mk. 8.34–38
32 Mk. 9.30, 31
33 Mk. 10.1
34 Lk. 9.51
35 e.g. Mk. 10.32–34, 45
36 see Lk. 9.51–18.14
37 Lk. 12.50
38 Lk. 18.31
39 Lk. 18.35–19.10
40 Jn. 7.2, 10, 14; 10.22, 23
41 Jn. 10.40; 11.54
42 Jn. 7.37–39; 8.12 and 9.5; 8.58; 10.11; 11.25, 26
43 Jn. 5.18; 7.30, 32; 8.59; 10.39; 11.53, 57
44 Mk. 2.1–3.6
45 e.g. Lk. 11.37–52
46 Mk. 7.1–13
47 Mk. 12.18–27
48 Lk. 19.41, 42
49 Zech. 9.9; Mt. 21.5
50 Mk. 11.15–19
51 Mk. 12
52 Mt. 23
53 Mt. 24; Mk. 13; Lk. 21
54 Jn. 12.20–33
55 Lk. 23.34; Jn. 19.26, 27; Lk. 23.43
56 Jn. 19.28; Mk. 15.33, 34; Jn. 19.30; Lk. 23.46
57 Lk. 23.46
58 Acts 2.42
59 Acts 2.14–40; 3.12–26; 5.29–32; 10.34–43

44

60 Acts 2.23
61 Acts 3–5
62 Acts 4.1, 2
63 Acts 5.41, 42
64 Acts 5.1–11
65 Acts 6.1–6
66 Acts 5.7
67 Acts 8.1–4
68 Acts 8.5–40
69 Acts 9.15
70 Acts 10, 11
71 Acts 10.47; 11.17;
15.7–11
72 Acts 11.19–26; 13.1–3
73 Gal. 4.13–15
74 The story of the first
missionary journey is
told in Acts 13.4 to
14.28
75 Acts 14.27
76 Acts 15.1, 5
77 Gal. 2.11–14
78 The Greek word
translated 'unchastity'
in Acts 15.20, 29 (RSV)
may refer to fornication
in particular, or to
immorality in general,
or (it has been argued)
to Jewish regulations
regarding marriage
within the prohibited
degrees.
79 The story of the second
missionary journey is
told in Acts 15.36–18.22
80 Acts 16.1–4; cf. 1 Cor.
9.19, 20
81 1 Thess. 3.1–5
82 1 Thess. 3.6; Acts 18.5
83 1 Thess. 1

84 1 Thess. 2
85 1 Thess. 5.14
86 The story of the third
missionary journey is
told in Acts 18.23–21.16
87 Acts 19.8–10
88 1 Cor. 1.4–9
89 1 Cor. 1.10–4.21
90 1 Cor. 5, 6
91 1 Cor. 11
92 1 Cor. 7
93 1 Cor. 8–10
94 1 Cor. 12–14
95 1 Cor. 15
96 2 Cor. 2.1
97 2 Cor. 1.12–14
98 2 Cor. 2.5–11
99 2 Cor. 3–6
100 2 Cor. 8, 9
101 2 Cor. 10–13
102 2 Cor. 12.14; 13.1
103 Acts 19.23–41
104 Acts 19.21, 22; 20.1, 2
105 Rom. 16.23; 1 Cor. 1.14
106 Rom. 1.8–15
107 Rom. 15.18–29
108 Rom. 1–3.20
109 Rom. 1.16; 3.22, 23;
10.12, 13 and also
chapters 9–11
110 Rom. 3.21–5.21
111 Rom. 6
112 Rom. 7.1–8.13
113 Rom. 8.14–39
114 Rom. 9
115 Rom. 10. See especially
verse 21
116 Rom. 11, especially
verses 12, 25 and 26
117 Rom. 12
118 Rom. 13

119 Rom. 14, 15
120 Acts 20.3–21.16
121 Acts 21.17–22.29
122 Acts 22.30–23.10
123 Acts 24.1–21
124 Acts 25.1–12
125 Acts 25.13–26.32
126 Acts 27.1–28.10
127 Acts 28.30, 31
128 Tit. 1.5
129 1 Tim. 1.3
130 Philem. 22
131 1 Tim. 1.3
132 Tit. 3.12
133 2 Tim. 4.13
134 2 Tim. 4.17
135 2 Tim. 4.7, 8
136 cf. 1 Pet. 5.13 where
    'Babylon' is almost
    certainly a symbol for
    Rome
137 1 Pet. 4.12
138 1 Pet. 4.13
139 1 Pet. 2.18–25
140 cf. 2 Pet. 2.19
141 Rev. 1.9
142 Rev. 22.20, 21

Have you seen
The Scripture Union
KEY BOOKS
Range?

UNDERSTANDING CHRISTIAN ATTITUDES
George Hoffman

The author deals positively and clearly with the Christian approach to a wide number of social and moral problems.

UNDERSTANDING THE SUPERNATURAL
Canon Stafford Wright

A timely assessment of the occult based on the warnings given in the Bible and the Christian's understanding of the power of Christ and the nature of evil.

UNDERSTANDING THE TEN COMMANDMENTS
John Eddison

The author considers the relevance of the Ten Commandments to contemporary life.

UNDERSTANDING OURSELVES
John Eddison

A sympathetic, Christian view of the anxiety and depression that trouble so many in today's world.

UNDERSTANDING THE WAY
Robinson and Winward

A practical guide to the Christian life.

UNDERSTANDING CHRISTIAN ETHICS
Gilbert Kirby

The principal of the London Bible College considers the application of Christian teaching in dealing with contemporary problems from euthanasia to pornography.

UNDERSTANDING BASIC BELIEFS
John Eddison

An outline of what Christians believe based on one of the great creeds of the Christian church.

LET'S TALK IT THROUGH
J. Hills Cotterill

Discussion starters and background material on a variety of topics from contemporary portrayals of Jesus Christ to the use of music in worship. A mine of information.

UNDERSTANDING LEADERSHIP
John Eddison

Ten studies on 'top men' of the Bible which aim to show exactly what the qualities are that make up a leader.

UNDERSTANDING GOD'S PLAN
David Howard

A very readable commentary on the great themes of the book of Job and their message for us in today's world.

UNDERSTANDING THE DEATH OF JESUS
John Eddison

A lively challenging look at the reasons why Jesus died on the cross and the implications of his death for us today.

UNDERSTANDING THE CHRISTIAN AND SEX
M. O. Vincent

A trained psychiatrist explores the role of sex in the life of the world and of the individual Christian.

DAILY BIBLE STUDY BOOKS

Thorough coverage of major Biblical passages combines scholarly insight with devotional warmth and practical experience. Studies of Biblical characters are also included.

Man separated from God	A. Skevington Wood
	E. M. Blaiklock
Jesus' Early Life	H. L. Ellison
	E. M. Blaiklock
Jesus' True Identity	James Philip
	E. M. Blaiklock
Man restored in Christ	W. L. Lane
	E. M. Blaiklock
God the Holy Spirit	Leon Morris
	E. M. Blaiklock
Christ Living with Him	J. I. Packer
	E. M. Blaiklock
God's Kingdom and Church	F. F. Bruce
	E. M. Blaiklock
Christ the Way to God	R. A. Finlayson
	E. M. Blaiklock

UNDERSTANDING THE NEW TESTAMENT

Based on Scripture Union's popular *Daily Bible Commentary* in four volumes these ten books offer a unique combination of daily Bible readings with the depth of a commentary.

St Matthew	F. F. Bruce
St Mark	I. H. Marshall
St Luke	E. M. Blaiklock
St John	R. E. Nixon
Acts	R. P. Martin
Romans	E. M. Blaiklock
1 Corinthians—Galatians	R. P.Martin
Ephesians—2 Thessalonians	W. L. Lane
1 Timothy—James	Leon Morris
1 Peter—Revelation	H. L. Ellison

SCRIPTURE UNION BIBLE DICTIONARIES

DICTIONARY OF BIBLE WORDS
John Eddison

John Eddison looks at a range of Bible words that are unfamiliar in everyday English and explains their original meaning and modern significance.

DICTIONARY OF BIBLE TIMES
Herbert Sundemo

With the help of maps, charts and over 200 line drawings the author covers, in one handy volume, topics ranging from geography to religious customs.

DICTIONARY OF BIBLE PEOPLE
J. Stafford Wright

Over 500 entries covering the major characters in the Bible. All the relevant facts of their lives are detailed and discussed in a lively, memorable style.

Your Own Personal Notes

52

Your Own Personal Notes

Your Own Personal Notes

54

Your Own Personal Notes

Your Own Personal Notes